Bugs and Other Creepy-Crawlies

Written by Tom Donegan
Reading consultants: Alan Howe and Christopher Collier,
Bath Spa University, UK

This edition published by Parragon Books Ltd in 2013 and distributed by

Parragon Inc.
440 Park Avenue South, 13th Floor
New York, NY 10016
www.parragon.com

Edited by; Grace Harvey
Designed by; Francesca Winterman and Kate Merritt
Production by; Joanne Knowlson

ISBN 978-1-4723-3025-3

Printed in China

Bugs and Other
Creepy-Crawlies

Bath · New York · Singapore · Hong Kong · Cologne · Delhi
Melbourne · Amsterdam · Johannesburg · Shenzhen

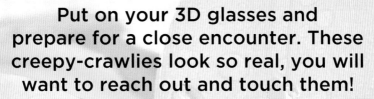

Put on your 3D glasses and prepare for a close encounter. These creepy-crawlies look so real, you will want to reach out and touch them!

Parents' Notes

This book is part of a series of nonfiction books designed to appeal to children learning to read. Each book has been developed with the help of educational experts.

At the end of the book is a quiz to help your child remember the information and the meanings of some of the words and sentences. Difficult words, which appear in bold in the book, can be found in the glossary at the back. There is also an index.

Contents

What Is a Bug?

We often call many different types of creepy-crawlies bugs, but they're not all the same.

Insects have six legs and two feelers on their forehead, called **antennae**. Dragonflies, beetles, butterflies, bees, wasps, and ants are all insects.

Spiders are not insects. They are **arachnids**. Arachnids have eight legs and no antennae.

Millipedes and centipedes have lots of legs and two antennae.

Insect

Spider

Millipede

Dragonfly

DISCOVERY FACT™

Insects, arachnids, millipedes, and centipedes do not have bones. Instead, their body is covered with a hard layer, called an **exoskeleton**.

Worker ants

DISCOVERY FACT™

Leafcutter ants can carry leaves that weigh 50 times as much as they do. That's like a man lifting a pickup truck.

Amazing Ants

Ants are insects that live in large groups called **colonies**.

A trail of ants

Most of the ants in a colony are worker ants. They build the nest, take care of the young, and look for food.

When a worker ant has found food, it returns to the colony. It leaves a smell trail on its way back, so that other ants can follow the trail to the food.

Queen ant

Each ant colony has a queen ant. She lays hundreds of eggs every day, so that the colony can grow.

Brilliant Beetles

Beetles live in forests, deserts, mountains, and lakes all around the world.

Most beetles have two pairs of wings. A beetle's shell opens to form the first pair, and the second pair, used for flying, is underneath.

Green beetle

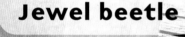

Jewel beetle

Beetles have hard jaws to carry and bite things, called mandibles. Male stag beetles use their giant mandibles to wrestle.

Some beetles are very bright and colorful, with beautiful patterns on their shells.

Ladybug

Stag beetles wrestling

DISCOVERY FACT™

Dung beetles roll the poop of other animals into large balls!

Bees and Wasps

Both bees and wasps have black and yellow stripes, buzzing wings, and sharp stingers. But if you look closely, you can spot the difference.

Bees have furry, round bodies, and wasps have smooth, slim bodies.

Both eat **pollen** and drink **nectar** from flowers. Honeybees collect nectar to make honey.

Bee

A bee can only sting once and then it dies, but a wasp can sting many times.

Wasp

Bee

Locusts are a type
of grasshopper.
Sometimes, millions
of hungry locusts
gather together
in huge groups,
called swarms.

Grasshopper

14

Crickets and Grasshoppers

Cricket

Jumping grasshopper

Crickets and grasshoppers both make chirping sounds by rubbing together parts of their body.

Crickets rub their wings together, and grasshoppers rub their legs against their wings.

Crickets and grasshoppers are very good jumpers, with long back legs that work like a spring. They can travel long distances in one leap!

Crickets have long, thin **antennae**, while grasshoppers have short, stubby antennae.

Butterfly Life Cycle

A beautiful winged butterfly starts its life as a little wriggly caterpillar.

First, a butterfly lays her egg on a leaf.

A caterpillar **hatches** from the egg and begins to eat the leaf.

When the caterpillar has eaten enough, it wraps itself up in a **cocoon**.

After two weeks or more, an adult butterfly comes out of the cocoon.

The butterfly dries its wings before it flies for the first time.

Butterfly eggs

Caterpillar

Cocoon

Butterfly

Butterfly

DISCOVERY FACT™

Every year, monarch butterflies travel from America and Canada to Mexico, to lay their eggs.

Super Spiders

From tiny money spiders to huge tarantulas, spiders come in many different sizes.

All spiders can squeeze silk thread out of silk **glands** on their stomachs.

Many spiders spin a web from silk to catch **prey**. Flies and other insects get trapped in the sticky web.

Fly trapped in a spiderweb

Spiders lay hundreds of eggs at once. They put them all in a silk pouch, called an egg sac. Some spiders carry their egg sac on their back to keep the eggs safe.

Wolf spider with egg sac

Spider

DISCOVERY FACT™

The black widow
spider is poisonous.
A bite from one can
make you very sick.

Goliath birdeater

DISCOVERY FACT™

Tarantulas shed their skin as they grow. This is called molting.

Terrifying Tarantulas

Tarantulas are large, hairy spiders. They live in warm places, such as jungles and deserts.

The goliath birdeater is the biggest tarantula of all. As well as eating small birds, it eats insects, frogs, and mice.

Mexican redknee

If attacked, the Mexican redknee kicks the spiky hairs off its back like arrows. These can be itchy if they get on your skin.

Greenbottle blue

Tarantulas have poor eyesight. The greenbottle blue uses the hairs on its legs to feel its way around.

Millipedes and centipedes look a lot alike, but they are actually very different.

Centipedes eat insects. They can move quickly and use **venom** to kill their **prey**.

Millipedes eat rotting leaves and other dead plants. They have shorter legs than centipedes and move slowly.

If attacked, a millipede will curl up into a tight spiral, with the head in the middle and its legs pulled underneath.

Millipede

Millipede curled into a spiral

Centipede

Bugs in Disguise

Some bugs are experts in disguise. Some use **camouflage** to hide from predators. Others pretend to be **predators** themselves!

Leaf insects disguise themselves as leaves. They even have a special way of walking that makes them look like a leaf being blown in the wind.

Stick insects look like sticks from the plants they live on. They even lay eggs that resemble plant seeds.

stick insect

Owl butterflies have marks on their wings that look like owl eyes. This scares predators away.

owl butterflies

Leaf insect

Quiz

Now try this quiz!
All the answers can be
found in this book.

1. How many legs
do insects have?

a) Four
b) Six
c) Eight

2. What do worker
ants leave behind to
tell other ants where
they have been?

a) A breadcrumb trail
b) A leaf trail
c) A smell trail

3. Which insect rolls the
poop of other animals?

a) Green beetle
b) Dung beetle
c) Ladybug

4. What do bees
and wasps feed on
from flowers?

a) Water and soil
b) Orange juice and wood
c) Nectar and pollen

5. What do caterpillars
wrap themselves in
when they are changing
into a butterfly?

a) Nest
b) Cocoon
c) Spiderweb

6. What do all
spiders produce?

a) Cotton
b) Wool
c) Silk

Glossary

Antennae   Two thin sensors on an insect's forehead, used to feel and sometimes to smell.

Arachnids   A group of animals, including spiders, scorpions, mites, and ticks.

Camouflage   A disguise—to take the same shape or color as the things around.

Cocoon   The hard shell made by a caterpillar to protect itself while it is turning into a butterfly.

Colony   A large group of insects living together in one or more nests.

Exoskeleton   A hard layer on the outside of the body that protects the organs inside.

Hatch   To break out of something.

Molting   Shed old skin or exoskeleton to make way for new growth.

Nectar	The sugary water made by flowers to attract animals.
Pollen	The fine yellow powder made by flowers.
Predator	An animal that hunts, kills, and eats other animals.
Prey	An animal that is hunted and killed for food by another animal.
Venom	A poisonous liquid made by some predators to help them kill or hurt their prey. Usually injected through teeth, fangs, or a sting.

Index

Acknowledgments

Main images:
pp22-23 Getty Images/John Mitchell

Inset images:
p15 Getty Images/Michael Durham

All other images from Shutterstock.